A New True Book

ARGENTINA

By Karen Jacobsen

Flag of Argentina

CHILDREN'S PRESS
A Division of Grolier Publishing
Sherman Turnpike
Danbury, Connecticut 06816

Argentine cowboys called
gauchos work on ranches.

PHOTO CREDITS

AP/Wide World Photos—33 (left), 34, 35 (left)

© Cameramann International, Ltd.—10, 15 (left), 37 (left), 40 (top left)

© Stuart Cohen—9 (right), 28, 42

© Victor Englebert—18 (left & bottom right), 39 (left), 40 (bottom left)

Reprinted with permission of *The New Book of Knowledge*, 1989 edition, © Grolier, Inc.—7

Historical Pictures Service, Chicago—24, 26, 29, 33 (right)

Nawrocki Stock Photo—© Mark Stevenson, 9 (left)

Odyssey/Frerck/Chicago—© Robert Frerck, 22, 40 (right), 44, 45 (2 photos)

© Chip and Rosa Maria de la Cueva Peterson—12 (2 photos), 13 (2 photos), 17, 20 (left)

Photri—11, 35 (right); © Charles Philip, 4 (2 photos), 15 (right)

Tom Stack & Associates—© Kevin Schafer, 15 (center)

Stock Imagery—© Fairchild, 25

SuperStock International, Inc.—© Shuster, Cover; © Pedro L. Raota, 2, 14 (right), 23; © Ann & Myron Sutton, 14 (left); © Kurt Scholz, 30

TSW-CLICK/Chicago—© Robert Frerck, 20 (right), 37 (right), 39 (right), 41 (left), 43

Valan—© Jean-Marie Jro, 16, 18 (top right); © Anthony Feist, 41 (right)

Cover—Harbor, Liberty Ave. Buenos Aires, Argentina

Library of Congress Cataloging-in-Publication Data

Jacobsen, Karen.
   Argentina / by Karen Jacobsen.
     p.   cm. — (A New true book)
   Includes index.
   Summary: Describes the geography, history, people, and culture of Argentina.
   ISBN 0-516-01101-4
   1. Argentina—Juvenile literature.
[1. Argentina.] I. Title.
F2808.2.J33 1990   90-36526
982—dc20   CIP
                         AC

TABLE OF CONTENTS

Great numbers of seals (above) and penguins come to Argentina's
Valdés Peninsula each summer to have their babies.

ARGENTINA IN THE WORLD

Look! Hundreds of whales! Thousands of seals! More than a million penguins! Every summer, all of these animals—and more—come to the Valdés Peninsula. They come to have their babies and spend the summer. The Valdés Peninsula sticks out into the Atlantic Ocean on the east coast of Argentina.

Argentina is the eighth largest country in the world. It lies south of the equator, in the southern half of South America. Argentina's name comes from the Latin word *argentum*, meaning "silver." Early Spanish explorers hoped to find silver in the new land.

Five countries share borders with Argentina. Chile

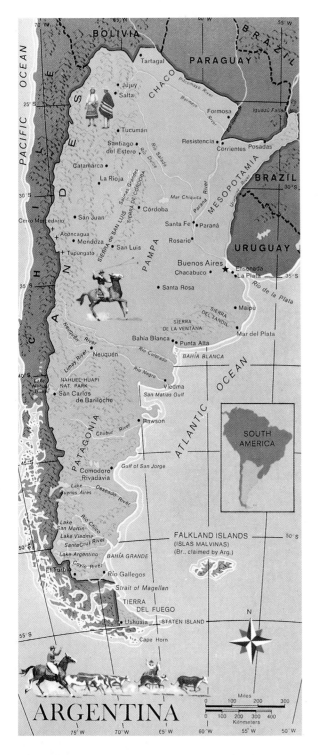

is in the west. Bolivia and Paraguay are in the north. Brazil, the largest country in South America, and Uruguay are in the northeast. The Atlantic Ocean is Argentina's border on the east.

ARGENTINA THE NATION

More than thirty-three million people live in Argentina. They are known as Argentines. Most Argentines speak the Spanish language.

Argentina is a republic. The government is run by a president and a Congress.

Buenos Aires is the capital of Argentina. *Buenos aires*

Tourists from all over the world come to enjoy the scenery, shopping, and fine restaurants in Buenos Aires.

means "fair winds" in Spanish. The people of Buenos Aires call themselves *porteños*, which means "people of the port."

Over twelve million people live in or around Buenos

The Avenida 9 de Julio in Buenos Aires is a street
named for Argentina's Independence Day, July 9.

Aires. It has many modern
skyscrapers, heavy traffic,
and busy people.

Argentina has four natural
regions—the Andes, the North,
Patagonia, and the Pampa.

THE ANDES

The Andes region covers
about one-third of Argentina.
The region is named for the
Andes Mountains that run
like a spine along western
Argentina.

Most of the land is too

The rugged peaks of the Andes Mountains form Argentina's border with Chile.

Wine grapes (left) are grown in irrigated vineyards.
The mountain pass of Las Cuevas, near the city of Mendoza (right)

steep or too cold for farming. But in the eastern foothills, people raise corn and grow grapes for wine.

There are several passes in the mountains. People use the passes to travel between Argentina and Chile. The city of Mendoza, Argentina, is built at the east of a major pass.

THE NORTH

Much of northern Argentina is flat land covered with grasses and forests. There are many rivers. In springtime, the rivers swell with rain and flood the swampy lowlands.

Argentina's many rivers flow through grasslands and forests.

A salt-mining operation (left) near Santa Rosa.
Cattle ranching (right) on the plains of northern Argentina

Summer, which lasts
from November to April in
Argentina, is hot and dry.
The floodwaters dry up and
leave salt on the land.

Ranchers in northern
Argentina raise cattle for
their meat and for their
hides, which are made into
leather.

14

Northern farmers grow cotton, fruit, rice, sugarcane, and yerba, a plant like tea. Its dried leaves are brewed in boiling water to make *maté*, a popular drink.

In the far north, there are rain forests. Jaguars, tapirs,

Rivers wind through the rain forests, which are the home of tapirs (center) and monkeys (right).

The magnificent Iguaçu Falls are two and one-half miles wide and from two hundred to three hundred feet high.

marsh deer, monkeys, and other wild animals live here. Small groups of Indians make their homes in the forests too.

At the border of Argentina and Brazil, on the Iguaçu River, are the Iguaçu Falls.

PATAGONIA

Patagonia is the southern region of Argentina. Along its Atlantic coastline, there are high cliffs and only a few harbors. In the west, there are canyons and sand dunes. Central Patagonia is a wide, grassy plateau. It is very dry and littered with stones.

An Atlantic beach on the Gulf of San Jorge in Patagonia

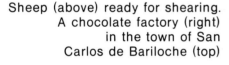

Sheep (above) ready for shearing.
A chocolate factory (right)
in the town of San
Carlos de Bariloche (top)

Patagonian sheep ranches
spread out over hundreds of
miles. Many of the sheep
ranchers have Welsh names.
They are the descendants of
settlers who came from Wales

in the 1860s.

In western Patagonia, the town of San Carlos de Bariloche is famous for fishing in summer, skiing in winter, and chocolate candy all year round.

Off the southern tip of Patagonia lies a group of islands called Tierra del Fuego. They are separated from the mainland by the Strait of Magellan. Western Tierra del Fuego belongs to Chile; eastern Tierra del Fuego belongs to Argentina.

THE PAMPA

North of Patagonia lies the Pampa, a large, fertile plain. Much of the Pampa is covered with grasses. The Pampa's rich soil grows wheat, fruits, and vegetables. Large herds of

The owners of *estancias* on Argentina's tall-grass prairies live in large *haciendas*.

cattle graze on the excellent pastures in the east.

Cattle ranches on the Pampa are called *estancias*. They sometimes cover hundreds of thousands of acres. Many people live and work on each *estancia*.

On the Pampa, the summers are warm and the winters mild. But sometimes there are wild storms with thunder and lightning. Cool, powerful winds called *pamperos* often follow the storms.

On special days, the gauchos wear traditional costumes.

GAUCHOS

The cowboys of Argentina are called *gauchos*. They are the descendants of early Indians and Spanish settlers. Long ago, gauchos hunted wild horses and cattle on the Pampa. Today, gauchos work for wages on *estancias*.

ARGENTINA'S PAST

Several tribes of Indians lived in Argentina when the first explorers arrived from Spain. Some tribes were wandering hunters. They

The *boleadoras* is still used by gauchos to catch cattle.

used spears or bows and arrows to hunt. They also had a special weapon called the *boleadoras*. It was made with two or three stones tied to leather thongs. It was twirled rapidly and thrown at the legs of an animal. The thongs wrapped around the legs and stopped the animal.

An early drawing of the Patagonian Indians

Other Indian tribes lived in villages. They raised animals and grew crops. They had many skills and crafts. Some dug long canals to irrigate their cornfields. Others used reeds to weave watertight boats for fishing and travel.

24

In 1516, a Spanish ship entered the Plata River. Its captain, Juan Díaz de Solís, and his crew were the first Europeans to explore the coast of Argentina.

In 1536, Pedro de Mendoza and some Spanish

This painting shows Pedro de Mendoza and his men arriving in Buenos Aires.

The site of Buenos Aires was chosen for the first permanent settlement in 1580 because of its natural harbor.

soldiers built a fort at Buenos Aires. But the Indians attacked and forced Mendoza to leave. After forty years, more Spanish arrived. In 1580, they built a new town at Buenos Aires.

In the 1600s, the Spanish king sold large pieces of land in Argentina to wealthy Spaniards. They sent settlers

to start *estancias* near
Buenos Aires. In 1776, Buenos
Aires was made the capital of
the Spanish Argentine colony.

In 1806, British soldiers
captured Buenos Aires. The
porteños armed themselves
and forced the British to leave.

The porteños decided
that they didn't want to be
ruled by Britain or Spain.
In 1810, Buenos Aires
declared its independence.

The people in the rest of
Argentina wanted to be
independent, too. But the

porteños refused to unite with the others.

Meanwhile, the Spanish army was preparing to attack Argentina.

But, the Argentine leader, José de San Martín, formed an army and defeated the Spanish troops. In 1816, Argentina was free of Spain.

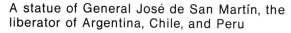
A statue of General José de San Martín, the liberator of Argentina, Chile, and Peru

INDEPENDENCE

De Rosas exiled
or killed his
enemies. He ran
the country
for his
own profit.

In 1828, Juan Manuel
de Rosas, a rich landowner,
seized power. He ruled
Argentina as a dictator for
more than twenty years.

Finally, in 1852, De Rosas
was forced to leave the
country. A year later,
Argentina had a constitution,
a president, and a new
capital at Paraná. Then, in
1862, Buenos Aires joined

The Capitol Building on the Plaza de Congrese, Buenos Aires

with the interior provinces
and became the capital of
a united Argentina.

Many changes followed
over the next half-century.
Roads, railroads, and

telegraph lines were built.
Thousands of immigrants
from Europe arrived each
year.

Argentina grew rich by
selling its grain and beef to
Europe. Then, in the early
1930s, the Great Depression
—a worldwide slump in
business—began. Other
countries could not afford to
buy products from Argentina.
Argentines lost their jobs
and went hungry.

MILITARY GOVERNMENT

In 1943, Colonel Juan Domingo Perón and some other military officers took over the government.

In 1946, Perón was elected president. He was popular with the working people. But, in 1955 Perón was overthrown by the military. He fled to exile in Spain.

In 1958, Argentina held its first free election in more than twenty years. Arturo

Juan Perón (left) resigned as president in 1955. Arturo Frondizi (right) became president in 1958. He was overthrown in 1962.

Frondizi was elected president. He led the country to develop new oil fields, a steel plant, and public housing projects. But, in 1962 the military again seized power.

Isabel Perón

During the 1960s and 1970s, there were strikes, protests, and violence.

To restore order, the military allowed Juan Perón to return from Spain. In 1973, Perón was elected president. When he died in 1974, his wife, Isabel Perón, became the new president of Argentina.

In 1976, the military arrested Isabel Perón and

again took over the

British naval forces (right) on the way to the Falkland Island war. Argentines laid claim to the islands, which they call *Islas Malvinas.*

government. A group called "the generals" ran the country. In 1982, the generals invaded the Falkland Islands, a British possession in the Atlantic Ocean off the coast of Argentina.

In a series of land, air, and sea battles, British forces recaptured the islands. The generals were disgraced. They resigned and elections were held.

Raúl Alfonsin was elected president. The nation had many problems. Argentina owed huge amounts of money to other countries. Workers were not paid for their work. Factories closed. People lost their jobs. Argentina's money was almost worthless.

In 1989, there were new elections. Carlos Saul Menem was elected president.

LIFE IN ARGENTINA

In Argentina, more than 90 percent of the people can read and write. By law, all children from six to fourteen years old must attend school. Education is free for elementary, high school, and

Elementary school students wear white smocks, called *delatales*, over their regular clothes. High school students (right) wear uniforms.

university students. But many students live in remote areas. They do not attend school because they live too far away.

Students go to high school for five years. Some take classes that prepare them for college. Others study business subjects or attend trade schools.

There are universities in many cities. The largest is in Buenos Aires. The oldest university is in Córdoba. It was started in 1613.

Left: The engineering building at the university in Buenos Aires.
Right: Gauchos are famous for their beef barbecues, called *asados*.

Some favorite Argentine foods are *empanadas*—pastries stuffed with meat or fruit; *carbonada criolla*—a thick soup made of meat, rice, potatoes, and onions; and *lacra*—an Indian stew of sausage, corn, and vegetables.

Artists gather in Buenos Aires' La Boca district (left), where the houses are gaily painted in contrasting colors. The tango is danced to music with an exciting beat (right).

Argentina has many artists. They produce paintings, sculpture, and fine crafts in leather, metals, clay, and woven fibers.

Argentine music and dance are known around the world. Most famous is the tango, a dramatic dance.

Argentine soccer teams compete in world-class tournaments. Polo players (right) hit the ball with a long mallet.

Soccer is the most popular sport in Argentina. Every neighborhood has a team. National teams play in large stadiums and compete in world championships.

Other popular sports are horse racing, polo, and *pato*.

The ball used in *pato* has handles so the players can pass it from one to another.

Like polo, pato is played
on horseback. The players
try to score baskets using a
six-handled ball.

Most Argentines are
Roman Catholics. Christmas,
Easter, and other Christian
holy days are national

holidays in Argentina. There are processions, feasts, dancing, and fireworks. During *Carnival*, a festival held before Lent, colorfully costumed Argentines dance in the streets.

An Indian procession in Buenos Aires honors a patron saint.

A stone monument called an obelisk is the symbol of Buenos Aires.

Other holidays recall important events in Argentine history. Argentines observe May 25 in honor of Argentina's first self-government (Buenos Aires, 1810). On July 9th they celebrate the independence of the republic (1816).

The story of Argentina has never been simple or easy. It is a nation with many problems. But it also has many strengths. Its people will make Argentina stronger and better than ever.

WORDS YOU SHOULD KNOW

argentum (ar • GEN • tum) — a Latin word meaning "silver"

boleadoras (bole • ee • ah • DOR • is) — a weapon of the Argentine Indians, used in hunting

Buenos Aires (BWAY • nohs AIR • res) — the capital city of Argentina

canyon (KAN • yun) — a deep valley with steep sides

carbonada criolla (kar • buh • NAH • dah kree • OH • la) — a thick soup

dictator (DIHK • tay • ter) — a ruler with total power

disgraced (dis • GRAYST) — shamed; discredited

Great Depression (GRAYT dih • PRESH • un) — a worldwide business slump in the 1930s during which many people lost their jobs

empanadas (em • pah • NA • das) — meat or fruit pies

equator (ee • KWAY • ter) — an imaginary line around the earth, equally distant from the North and South poles

estancia (ess • TAHN • see • ya) — an Argentine cattle ranch

Falkland Islands (FAWK • land EYE • lends) — British-owned islands off the coast of Argentina

foothills (FOOT • hilz) — hills at the base of a mountain range

gaucho (GOW • cho) — an Argentine cowboy

Iguaçu River (ee • GWAH • soo) — a river in northeastern Argentina

immigrants (IM • ih • grints) — people who came to a country to settle

irrigate (EER • ih • gait) — to bring water to crops by means of ditches or channels

jaguar (JAG • wahr) — a large wild spotted cat

lacra (LAH • kra) — an Indian stew

marsh deer (MARSH DEAR) —large deer that live in swampy
  plains and forests
maté (mat • AY) —a type of tea made from yerba leaves
pamperos (pom • PAYR • ohs) —strong, cool winds that blow on
  the Pampa
Patagonia (pat • ah • GO • nee • ya) —a region in southern
  Argentina
pato (PAH • to) —a game played on horseback with a six-handled
  ball
plateau (plat • OH) —an area of elevated flat land
porteños (por • TAYN • yoss) —a nickname for the people who
  live in Buenos Aires
province (PRAH • vince) —a section of a country, like a state in the
  United States
soccer (SAHK • er) —a game in which one team tries to kick a
  large ball into the opposing team's goal
tango (TANG • oh) —a slow, dramatic dance
tapir (TAY • peer) —a large mammal that looks like a pig with a
  long snout
yerba (YER • bah) —a tree whose leaves are made into a tea
  called maté

INDEX

About the Author

Karen Jacobsen is a graduate of the University of Connecticut and Syracuse University. She has been a teacher and is a writer. She likes to find out about interesting subjects and then write about them.